Writing A Book
The Seven "P's" to Becoming an Author

By
Amazon Best-Selling Author

David Jeffers

Table of Contents

WELCOME!

If you're reading this book, then you've at least have a passing interest in becoming a published author. My hope is that by time you finish reading this book, you will be bound and determined to fulfill your dream of not only writing a book, but also actually seeing it in print.

I cannot tell you the thrill I experienced when I received a copy of my first book back in 2006. The sense of personal achievement and validation was overwhelming. Since my first book, I've become an Amazon best-selling author writing pamphlets on politics and religion, published a 10-volume devotional series (with the last two set for publication in 2017), and co-authored a book on overcoming grief. Please take time to visit my Amazon author page (http://amzn.to/2gh7Gy2) so you can see that it is very possible to put out a large volume of work while holding down a full-time job.

Why do I mention the full-time job? It is because most aspiring authors have full-time jobs but dream of becoming a successful author. If you're like me, part of the dream of being an author is being able to dedicate your life to creating content that adds value to people's lives. If that is you, then you will recognize the purpose of this book.

My heart's desire and prayer is that by time you're done reading this book, you will have before you a roadmap to finally publishing your book. You will actually set out to becoming not only a published author, but also a best-selling one.

Now this is not a guarantee that you will become a best-selling author, but if you master the seven P's in this book, you will know what it takes. The success of your book will be determined by its content and your commitment to it becoming a best-seller.

Imagine seeing your name and book on the Amazon best-seller list in your particular category. You can achieve this goal with determination and hard work.

I invite you to follow the seven-step process of the seven "P's": Passion, Pursuit, Preparation, Practice, Planning, Publishing, and Promoting.

Enough of the chit chat; let's get started!

Passion
Passion propels your dreams…

What is the secret to becoming a successful author? It is none other than being passionate about your subject. There are many authors who write for a living, but they long ago lost their passion for their subject. It has become nothing more than a job. Sound familiar?

Perhaps you have a job that you are thankful for because it helps to provide for your family. However, there is something missing. You may have never been really excited about your line of work, but you were grateful to have a job with a good salary and benefits package.

Nevertheless, you've never been passionate about your vocation. You find yourself daydreaming about someday becoming a successful author. Then you snap yourself out of your temporary trance and get back to the "old grindstone."

If that describes you, then that is actually the first step to becoming a published author!

The Secret Ingredient

If you do not have passion, then you are not going to become a published author. You definitely won't if you are working 9 to 5 at your regular job. Why is passion so important?

It is because nothing excites us more than our passions.

As I write this, I just got my second cup of coffee at 6:30 in the morning. I'm writing this *before* I go to my day job.

Why am I doing this?

First, I want to show you that you can find time in your day to make progress on fulfilling your dream.

Second, and more importantly, it is because I am passionate about helping prospective authors finally becoming published.

It has taken me ten years to discover what I have learned, and I know if I told you it would take you ten years to get where I am, most of you would quit.

However, I don't want you to quit, and neither do you. I know you have a deep desire to accomplish your dream of becoming a published author.

I had and have that same deep desire and I would gladly spend ten years pursuing my dream again. I would do so because I discovered something exciting along the way.

Passion Brings Expertise

I want you to think about a hobby or subject of which you are very knowledgeable. You could even humbly admit that you are somewhat of an expert on said hobby or subject.

How did you become such an expert in your field?

It is because of your passion for it, right?

If we will pursue our passion, we can't help but to become an expert. That should greatly excite you! Why?

You can be excited about it because you may already be thinking that you are not qualified to become an author. After all, you have no formal training. You never attended college or even took a course on writing (um, that's the purpose of this book!).

You may have poor grammar skills and a limited vocabulary. Okay, then well goodbye!

STOP! I'm just kidding. I was momentarily joining you in your pity party.

I'm not making light of any real limitations you may have. However, know this: every limitation can be overcome by passion.

Of course, there are exceptions to this. Passion for singing will not make you a singer. Just watch the American Idol auditions for examples of that truth.

Understand that what you lack are writing skills, skills that can be learned. There are tools available to you that will help you master these skills.

I'm going to share some of those tools in the preceding pages, but I want you to flush your thoughts of any negativity because of your limitations.

I want your mind steeled for this journey of becoming a published author.

I need to you do something before we go to the next chapter. I want you to fill in the blank in the sentence below. Go ahead, I'll wait.

My great passion is _____

and I am ready to become a published author on this subject.

You got it? Excellent!

It's way past time we pursue that passion...

Pursuit
Pursue your passion…

What is it that you are passionate about? My passions are baseball, the Bible, and history. As a kid growing up, I knew every starting lineup of every Major League baseball team.

I have jokingly say that if the MLB channel had been around when I was younger, I'd still be living in my Mom's basement. Okay, that's not entirely accurate because we didn't have a basement, but you get the picture. I have had a love affair with baseball for over 50 years.

So, have I ever written on baseball? No, but I know enough about the game that I could write about it. However, baseball has taken a back seat to my other two passions. As I wrote in the introduction, I have a devotional series and numerous pamphlets on history, particularly about the relationship religion played on America's founding.

I am so passionate about the Bible that I earned a bachelor's degree in religion and a master of arts in theological studies. I hungered for not only biblical knowledge, but also and more importantly, biblical wisdom. I love teaching Sunday school and writing about the revelations God gives me during my Bible study.

My devotional series is titled, *Eavesdropping on God: One Man's Conversations with the Lord.* It all began quite innocently. It was a few days into January 2008, and I felt the Lord prompting me to write a devotional. I titled it, *How Are You Doing?* It was probably 300-400 words, somewhat amateurish in comparison to my later work, and I sent it to about 40 people.

To date I have written more than 1000 devotionals that average 650 words and have over 230 subscribers (I'll provide a link for you to subscribe at the end of this chapter). How did I go from a

—

seemingly innocuous start to a soon-to-be 12-volume series? I pursued it!

The Secret Ingredient

The secret to becoming a published author is to pursue that which excites you. Perhaps at this point you don't think you have any passions. Let me help you with that. Causes and hobbies often become passions.

If you are involved in charitable work; that is most likely your passion. If you have a hobby, then you no doubt pursue it with at least some degree of passion.

Need me to prove it to you?

If I asked you why you are involved in a certain cause, and secretly recorded your answer, I bet you would be surprised at the level of your passion. You are probably not aware of how passionate you are about your cause. How is that possible? It is because you are so wrapped up in it that you don't have time to evaluate your level of passion.

I'll have you figure that out here in a few. But for now, start mentally-picturing yourself explaining why you are involved in your particular cause.

If not a cause, is there a hobby that you enjoy? Like my baseball, are you a fanatic (aka fan) for a particular sport? Do you enjoy a particular arts or crafts? My wife is a very "craftsy" person and I'm always amazed at her near-perfectionist detail to anything she creates. She is that way because she is passionate about making beautiful things for other people. She has turned her craft into a cause. She loves to serve others.

Maybe that is your passion. You love to serve others. You have a servant heart. You have been serving in your local church and/or charity for years now and have become an expert in that particular endeavor. How did you become an expert? You pursued your passion.

Maybe at this point you realize that you're more like me; you have three passions. That's good! Take the time to write them down. Yes, do so right now, below:

My three passions are...
1. _____

2. _____

3. _____

You might actually have more than three, but let's keep the list short because now you have to choose one (OH NO!). The choice you need to make is the one passion you feel the most comfortable explaining. Again, imagine you have to explain to me why you are so passionate about a certain subject. That is going to become your pursuit to publish. Go ahead, make the decision:

My great passion is _____

and I am ready to become a published author on this subject.

Hey wait a minute! I filled that out in the last chapter. Did you come up with the same passion? Good! Just checking. I wasn't tricking you, I was just making sure. Why? It is because the next step is why many would-be authors never become published.

It is time to get to work. It is time to prepare...

<u>Preparation</u>
Preparation is key…

So, you may be feeling really good about yourself because you realize that you are an expert at something. Before your head swells to the next hat size, let me give you a dose of reality.

<u>Expertise Takes Work</u>

This uncomfortable fact is not meant to discourage you; quite the contrary. It is the practical first step you are going to take in publishing your book. Most wannabe authors think they can just sit down in front of a computer or grab a pencil and notepad and start writing a book.

Those books are rarely published and it is because of one often overlooked lesson in writing. Streams of consciousness make for poor writing.

What do I mean by this?

Most people I know who want to become authors believe their life story would make a best seller. I need to dispel this myth right now; that is rarely the case.

Like, hardly ever is someone's life story a best-seller, particularly if you are not already famous. So why is that?

It is because your life story is not all that different than most people. Oh, sure, the events in your life may be somewhat different, but to be honest, you're just living life, just like everyone else.

If you want to be a great author, then you need to understand a very important secret.

Experts Study!

Now before you put this book down to forever become a dust magnet, let me give you a surprising fact. You've already begun studying your area of expertise. Remember that two (and exactly alike) sentences I had you complete in the previous two chapters?

That passion that you are ready to turn into a book didn't become a passion because you have a passing interest in it. You have already spent time learning about your field of expertise and have acquired a wealth of knowledge about it.

But guess what? Your passion may already have book written about it. Oh, no, I'm too late!

Not at all.

Experts Synthesize

What do I mean by *synthesize*? You've probably already done this without knowing it, but you may already have a collection of articles, books, pamphlets, and/or websites that provide information on your area of expertise.

This is good! That's where I want you to start. Go back and read all the information you've already gathered on your subject. Read and read it again. I want you to digest it. Be sure to write down any thoughts that come to mind as you are reading your material.

Once you complete that, I want you to get at least five more sources in your area of expertise. Wash, rinse, and wash again. Meaning, I want you to read and read again the new material, however this time around don't take notes until the second reading.

Once you have accomplished this task you will have more information than you ever imagined. Now of course you don't have to stop at five new sources, but I want you to use that as a minimum. If in your information search you find numerous sources that interest you, then by all means use them. Just be careful of information overload.

Once last thing; I know I said in my introduction that I pursued my Bible passion into obtaining a bachelor's and master's degree. You do not have to have a degree in your area of passion to be an expert.

You just need to be committed to your passion.

And as a sign of that commitment, I want you to write down the titles of the five new sources you obtain for your preparation. You can move to the next chapter before you finish this task, but be sure to come back and fill this out.

However, if you're serious about this, you could accomplish this first!

1. _____

2. _____

3. _____

4. _____

5. _____

Practice
Practice makes perfect...

You are not a writer because you write. You write because you are a writer. I want that to be the underlying motivation in your pursuit of becoming a published author. That being said, there is a discipline you must master (stay with me!).

Writers Write!

If you want to be a writer, you have to write! I know I just said you are not a writer because you write. However, you cannot be a writer if you do not write. It may seem that I'm mastering the obvious, but I cannot tell you how many wannabe writers I know who have never written or have done very little writing.

On the flip side, I have a very good friend whom I am trying to get to start a blog. Just in case you do not know, a blog is short for weblog, a web log. Most of you may have a few blogs you regularly visit. You can visit my two main blogs at www.saltandlightblog.com and www.thetruthwatch.org to get some ideas of what blogs look like. The latter page contains a blog but also provides other information.

Back to my friend...he is a prolific writer without realizing it. He publishes great content almost every day on his Facebook page and in response to other posts he reads. However, he does not have his own blog, of which I've been trying to encourage him to start. I've even offered to host his blog just to get him started.

It is frustrating to see such great content being limited to Facebook posts. Why is this so frustrating? Unless you know of someone, I don't know of any authors who began their writing career after being discovered on Facebook. Facebook is a great platform to share your writing, such as a blog. However, social media is an excellent platform to share their writing from other sources. It should not be the sole source.

So how do you get started writing?

Writer Platforms

I have already mentioned starting a blog. In case you don't think you can pull this off, a young lady from my church has a blog titled *Emma Elizabeth* and she's been blogging for almost a year. I encourage you to visit her blog to get an idea of how an aspiring writer can easily put out excellent content, and do so free of charge:

Visit: https://eelizabethb.wordpress.com

What you will notice is how much Emma's writing has improved over the year. There is a reason for that and it is the subtitle of this chapter, *Practice Makes Perfect*. More on that in a bit.

If you are not yet ready to blog, another outlet that you can use free of charge and get noticed locally is to write letters to the editor of your hometown newspaper. This is an excellent outlet for two reasons.

First, it allows you to publish content that is important to you and relevant to key issues concerning current events.

Second, it requires you to organize your thoughts in a coherent manner. If you have already published some letters to the editor, I want you to go back and read those. Evaluate them for content and style. If you have been doing this for a while, you should discover a level of improvement.

If you haven't done so, I want you to do something this week. I want you to either respond to a news article in your local paper, or to a current event and write a letter to the editor. Visit their page and submit it to the editor. You can do so easily through email. Be sure to read their publishing requirements, such as word count and font usage. Not reading the publishing requirements is the quickest way to have your content rejected.

Perhaps you are thinking on a grander scheme. You already have a blog or that just doesn't seem to fit your writing style. Have you ever considered publishing a newsletter? Newsletters are excellent platforms for writing in a specialized field.

I publish a weekly newsletter titled *The Truth* where we look at one issue in politics through a biblical lens. It is four pages:

Page One is where I write a short column titled *Unshackled*, it is an opinion piece.

Page Two is *From the Founders* where I look at the original intent of the Founding Fathers in relation to the current topic.

Page Three is *From the Pulpit* where I look at the current topic through a biblical lens. I find content from past sermons that help put the issue in a biblical perspective.

Page Four is *To the Streets* where I give my readers actual steps they can take to affect change in the current topic. Guess what? One of the things I often encourage them to do is write letters to the editor.

A newsletter is an excellent platform to not only publish your excellent content and serve your reader, but you can also charge an annual subscription for it.

I actually can help you set up a blog or newsletter in my coaching program, of which I'll share with you at the end of this book.

Writer's Wisdom

Before we move on to the last three chapters, which by the way are the nuts and bolts of becoming a published author, I want to close this chapter with two important things I've learned in the last ten years of writing.

It was actually about 13 years ago when I started my first blog, *Right Face*. When I think about it, it was really quite simple and primitive. I not only shared my writing, but that of others. The writer who encouraged me to begin a blog was my dear friend Greg Allen. Greg is a prolific writer who used to host the excellent radio show *The Right Balance.*

Greg shared with me a nugget of writer wisdom that I etched into my writer's soul. He told to not love or hate my writing. He said that would help limit pride when I am successful and hurt when I am rejected. I have relied on that wisdom more times than I can remember.

The second important thing I want to share with you is a note of encouragement, and I'll even call it a promise.

The more you write, the better writer you become!

Remember *Emma Elizabeth*? Go back and read some of her content. Begin in January 2016, read a couple of post, jump down to July 2016 and do the same. Then go to her last two posts and read those. You will see how strong her writing has become over the past year.

That is because, yep you guess it...

The more you write, the better writer you become!

I want you to complete the following sentence:

Today I will begin to write by

_____

_____

_____ .

You should have written *starting a blog or newsletter, writing a letter to the editor,* or you can even say *writing my book.*

So, you are ready to pursue your passion of becoming a published author, you've prepared and even practice some.

Now it's time to get serious. It's time to come up with a manuscript.

I know, right! This is both exciting and terrifying.

The next chapter is going to corral that excitement, overcome the terror, and prevent you from just writing boring and unorganized streams of consciousness.

It's time to plan...

Planning
Outline your story...

Now that you have gathered all your information, you are going to need to organize it. No doubt you've found more information with which you know what to do. Or perhaps you think you do not have enough information.

This is where planning becomes your friend. An outline is going to help you put the various pieces of information into data clusters. Data clusters are groups of info nuggets that have the same theme or topic.

What if you're not sure which nugget belongs in a particular cluster? Here's a little exercise that will help you get started.

Mindmapping

Either grab pen and paper, or sit down before your computer, and just start writing on your subject. Now this might seem like you're writing streams of consciousness, but you're actually writing out everything you can think of on your topic. Remember, you have compiled a lot of information, and much of it is etched into your brain.

Mindmapping is a way of unlocking all the knowledge stored in your head. The key is to not try to organize your thoughts and come up with a manuscript ready for publication. You're putting down on paper all the knowledge you have on your topic.

Experts do this all the time, some without realizing they're doing so. Whenever you're going to tackle an issue or a problem, the best question you can ask initially is, "What do we know so far?" This allows you to discover the facts you know and also how much information is missing.

Mindmapping for a writer does the same thing. If I am interested in writing on a subject, I use this technique.

I'll use my newsletter *The Truth* as an example. I am interested in writing on a particular political issue. I will actually grab pencil and paper and start writing my opinion piece for my *Unshackled* column.

Mind you, I don't just pluck a topic out of thin air. It is something that is relevant to current events that I've been tracking to some degree. However, I may not have all the facts, but I sure do have an opinion (sound familiar?).

I want to capture my thoughts and feelings on the topic to see if I even have something to pursue. If I have been following the issue, usually I have plenty to say about it. However, even if I've been tracking it closely, I always discover information that I need to gather or confirm. Mindmapping is my most valuable writing tool.

Whether your research and/or the mindmapping exercise is how you get started, once you do, you will have to organize all this information into data clusters.

For the sake of time and space, I won't go it great detail on the step-by-step process, but I'm sure you've got a good idea of where to get started. I do cover the step-by-step process in my coaching program, but if you've ever written a research paper, you should have enough to get started.

So, let's use the next tool in the writer's toolbox, an outline.

The Roadmap

I highly encourage you to use an outline. This outline is discovered through Mindmapping or data clustering. Either way, you should be able to set a course for your writing, like a roadmap.

Sometimes, such as one book I'm working on now, you may come up with a table of contents before you do any real research or mindmapping. How does this happen?

You know your subject and you already have numerous subtopics. You come up with a title for your book, and write out the areas you want to cover. That list becomes your table of contents. A table of contents is an excellent outline.

Guess what? The reverse is true. Your outline can become your table of contents.

No matter how you organize your information, now is when the real progress begins.

The Writer's Road

One recommendation before we go on. After you have developed your outline, I highly recommend you leave it for a day. Come back to it fresh and you'll validate that the outline is the roadmap you want to follow.

An outline minimizes frustration, and reattacking it the next day confirms that the trip you're about to begin is the one you want to take.

Each main heading in your outline should be a main point of your topic. If it is not, then it may be better suited as a supporting point. Under each main point, you will write a bullet statement.

Bullet statements are key road signs because these will become your paragraphs. Be sure to capture as many of these as possible. Don't get "wrapped around the axle" trying to reorganize these bullet statements.

What I mean by this, is you may be down the road a bit, write a bullet statement and realize that it should have been under a different main point. You can jot a quick note next to it, but don't stop writing your bullet statements to reorganize your outline. You can do that later.

I cannot emphasize this point enough. I have been guilty of going down this rabbit hole and it has greatly hindered my creativity. Overcome the urge to organize while you're either mindmapping or writing your outline. Organize after you've captured the information.

Destination Dreamland!

Dreamland? What do I mean by that? You've longed dreamed of becoming a writer and now you have a completed outline, complete with bullet statements.

Time to write!

Take your outline and start writing. Write, write, write.

You should spend at least one hour a day writing. In one hour, you can write anywhere from 300 to 1000 words. You'll be able to do so because you have done all the grunt work ahead of time. Your outline shows you the way.

You should be able to complete one chapter a day. That is what I've done with this book. I've worked for about an hour each morning to come up with each chapter. My outline is the webinar you watched that led you to this book. If you haven't seen the webinar yet, you can do so at www.7ps2authorship.com.

Once again, I want to emphasize that you not spend too much time editing. As a practice, I do read the previous chapter before I begin the next. It reignites my brain and I can quickly edit any mistakes I discover. However, I read to reignite more than edit. Be sure that you make that your main effort.

There are a number of ways you can edit your completed manuscript. You can ask a couple of friends to read it and not only point out any errors, but also any areas of confusion. Just be sure you don't prejudice them by explaining the manuscript to them in detail. Let them do their own discovering.

You can also hire a proofreader at either www.fiverr.com or www.elance.com for a pretty reasonable price. If you hire me as a coach, then I'll be sure to proofread your manuscript myself and get two others to help me.

No matter how you do your proofreading, be sure you make a great effort in getting this right. You must plan time for proofreading in the process of getting published. It is in fact the most important step in publishing, other than actually getting published.

Which is our next step...

Publishing
Your dream coming true...

Getting published can be either the easiest or most difficult part of the process. The latter will be if you try to sign on with a publishing company. For that to happen, you will have to have a literary agent. It is very difficult, but not impossible, to get hired on with an agent. However, the competition is extreme and it takes a great deal of effort, frustration, and commitment to find an agent. Finding an agent is not actually a guarantee of getting published. It just means your manuscript will get in front of some publishers.

I'm not telling you this to discourage you. If you are intent on selling your book to a publishing company, then there are some resources available to you. I highly recommend you purchase Jeff Herman's *Guide to Book Publishers, Editors, & Literary Agents: Who they are! What they want! How to win them Over!* Even if you decide to not take the traditional path to publishing, this book is still an excellent resource.

Self-Publishing

The new kid in town in the publishing world is self-publishing. For a while, on-demand publishing was the alternative to traditional publishing. However, self-publishing is the no-cost method. With on-demand you are still paying a publishing company a fee. Now you get a few more incentives for the price, but it will usually run you in the hundreds if not thousands.

My first book, *Understanding Evangelicals: A Guide to Jesusland* was initially published through Xulon Press, a fine Christian publishing company. However, it cost me a couple of thousands of dollars to use their services. Additionally, you have to pay an annual fee to keep your book available through their company.

I am publishing that book the same way I've done my subsequent books: self-publishing.

This can literally be no cost to you. You can have your book published on Amazon, Barnes and Noble, and iBooks in both print and e-reader, for no cost. However, you must be able to correctly format your books, both cover and manuscript, to meet the publishing standards.

Hiring Free-Lancers

Each publishing company outlines their specific publishing standards so if you have advanced editing skills in word-processing and photo-shopping you can easily meet those standards. I do not so I use www.fiverr.com to do all those editing task.

I do initially create my own book covers, either from photos I own or purchase at www.istockphoto.com, where you purchase publishing rights of photos. I use PowerPoint to develop my covers and then save them as a jpeg file.

There are minimal pixel requirements that each company has, so you'll have to be sure you meet those. I use www.resizeyourimage.com to get the correct size for my cover. You will have to develop a back cover also. This is why I use a free-lancer because I'm not skilled enough to combine the front, back, and spine of a cover into one pdf file. My graphics artist can knock out a book cover in just a few hours that meets the publishing standards.

I also hire a free-lancer to format my manuscript into files that can be published in every format; print, Kindle, Nook, and iBooks. The cost of formatting is dependent upon the size of your manuscript; however, it can usually be done for around $50.

My usual total cost of formatting my cover and manuscript is less than $100. That is a sight better than what I paid with my first book.

<u>Publishing Avenues</u>

Imagine seeing your book on Amazon, Kindle, B&N Nook, or iBooks! You're almost there, however you will have to open a free account with each publishing outlet. I highly recommend you begin at Amazon. There are three things to do there.

1. Open an account at www.createspace.com. This is Amazon's self-publishing print service. They print on-demand at no cost to you. Amazon simply takes its cut from the price of the book, and you get the rest in royalties. This is far more lucrative than traditional publishing. Understand that you will have to do your own marketing. Will cover that in the next chapter.
2. Open an account at www.kdp.amazon.com. This is where your book will be made available on Kindle e-readers. CreateSpace can publish your book to Kindle, but I prefer to keep these separate. One reason is that I publish short pamphlets that usually don't meet the minimum page requirement to be printed on CreateSpace. I just like keeping both separate.
3. Create your own Amazon.com author page at www.authorcentral.amazon.com. You can track your sales, upload book trailers (more on that in the next chapter), and add all your published Amazon books in one place.

You will need to also open a free account at Barnes and Noble for their print and e-reader services and at www.smashwords.com. The latter offers only eBook services, but is another valuable publishing avenue.

I actually want you to go and open accounts at each of the websites I've listed. I want you to do so now. Oh, but Dave, I don't have a manuscript yet! I know, but if you are truly serious about becoming a published author, I want you to go ahead and open all the publishing avenues now. This is a step of faith and determination to make your dream a reality.

By opening accounts at each publishing avenue, you are making the commitment to get to work! So many prospective authors never get published because they use the excuse of not being able to find a publisher. Well dear friend, you are going to be your own publisher!

With becoming your own publisher comes the added and challenging task on becoming your own book promoter.

Go to the page and let's learn how...

Promoting
Finding your audience...

As a creator, you are a writer. As an author, you are an entrepreneur. Your book is your business; it is your calling card. Promoting your business is where the hard work really begins. All businesses come down to one thing: marketing.

As Brian Tracy likes to say, marketing makes selling unnecessary. While I do not have a degree in either business or marketing, I have studied many great entrepreneurial marketers because I know that if I want to become a full-time author, then I am going to have to sell books.

If you're already getting a sour taste in your mouth, go get a mint. This is not going to be as difficult or unsavory as it may sound. You may already have some marketing avenues and you don't even know it. Let me show you how.

Blogs versus Websites

If you don't already have a blog, I suggest you get one. You can make it solely about the book you've written or are going to write. I don't recommend that you have a website that is solely dedicated to selling your book. That's what your Amazon author page does.

A blog can be the title of your book or the subject. I have a blog that you have already been to if you watched the free webinar. However, I also blog there. I write little posts there that allow me to express ideas about writing and encourage other writers. It also allows me to post webinars and other media outlets. I'm considering starting a podcast too, if I see a need to fill.

Oh, and I also make my book available too.

Plus, I have other products available or coming soon, such as live events and audio lessons.

You can get a blog for free just by doing an online search for free blog hosting. However, I recommend you go through a webhosting company; I use bluehost.com.

With a webhosting company, you can come up with a unique web address, for instance mine is www.7ps2authorship.com. The web address should be relative to your book or subject and easy to remember.

Once you get your web address, you can use either WordPress (which I highly recommend for blogging) or Weebly for just setting up a website. In my coaching program, I set this all up for you, but you can do this on your own. Bluehost has excellent tutorials and live online help to assist you. They will even set up your blog for a reasonable fee.

(For the record, I am receiving no compensation for any of the recommendations I make in this book.)

Email List

You may not be aware of the fact that one of the tried and true marketing techniques resides on your email provider. If you have an address book with email addresses of friends, relatives, associates, and neighbors, then you have an email list.

An email list is a great marketing tool because it allows you to notify people close to you that you have a book. One of the marketing gurus I've studied under is Jeff Walker. Jeff has an amazing story and his book *Launch* is a must have. More importantly, Jeff puts out weekly vlogs (video blogs) on marketing. I highly recommend you visit his website www.jeffwalker.com. You're going to fall in love with Jeff!

What's also nice about email is you can get those on your list to forward your email to those on their list and help spread the exciting news about your book.

Never underestimate the value of an email list, no matter its size.

Bottom line: use your list!

Social Media

See, I told you that you already had a marketing avenue, maybe more than one. Facebook is probably the most notable social media outlet and if you don't have a Facebook account, you need to get one. You can actually have an author page dedicated to your writing. Facebook is great because you can get immediate feedback on all your writing.

You can post your blog link, make your book available to buy, and run ideas by your audience. You can set up a survey, get feedback on cover ideas or put multiple cover ideas and let your friends help you choose.

Think of Facebook as a community for readers, where you can find readers that are interested in your genre, allowing you to focus your efforts on your most likely customers. If thinking of your Facebook friends as your customers makes you uncomfortable, understand their buying your book is an outcome, not the reason for the relationship.

LinkedIn, Google Plus, Twitter, Pinterest, YouTube, and numerous other social media outlets are all excellent marketing resources for you to use. As a minimum, I recommend you have a Facebook, LinkedIn, and Twitter account.

Book Tours

There are two types of book tours: traditional and virtual. We'll look at each a little closer.

Traditional book tours mean going to book stores for signings and speaking engagements. Your local book store is always looking for an author signing. Offer them to give a brief presentation with a question and answer period, and then sell your books either on consignment or better yet, the bookstore will already have them in stock.

The former means you bring a box of books and they take a cut for every book they ring up. The latter means they ordered your books and you've already received the royalties. Obviously, the latter is the preferred method. Either way, do not be disappointed if you do not sell lots of books. Twenty books sold is a good book signing for your first time. The main point is to promote your book.

You can also offer to do speaking engagements for no cost to the host at your local library and the various community clubs, such as the Chamber of Commerce, Rotary Club, or any local writer's groups. Be sure to search your local area for these types of avenues. Word of mouth is a great way to gain momentum and notoriety as a new author.

As a segue to the virtual book tour, be sure to contact your local radio station prior to your book signing. Offer them a good interview about your book and promote your book signing. This helps both the radio station and local book store. You can send them a copy of your book with suggested questions for them to ask. As an occasional radio host, I appreciate receiving these suggested questions.

A virtual book tour comes in different forms. You can use virtual meeting places to perform live tours, such as Google Hangouts or Facebook Live. These are great for your audience to get to know you better. If you're doing a live event online, I recommend you keep it to 30-60 minutes. You should spend no more than 15 minutes explaining the book; its genesis, the writing process, and any challenges and victories you experienced.

The last 15-45 minutes can be dedicated to question and answers. Attendees love to be a part of a live event if questions can be asked. I've got some great questions that have actually help hone my presentation, make me discover more things about myself as an author and creator, and given me topics to explore for a possible new book.

A webinar is an excellent source for a virtual tour. This can actually be your best tool because you can record it and make it available on your blog or website and at your Amazon author page. This way your readers can visit it anytime and as many times as they like.

Book trailers are also a great way to advertise your book. You can hire a freelance producer for this or develop one yourself if you have movie-making skills. I also cover this in my coaching program and can even produce one for you, if you desire.

This is just a few examples of how you can get your face in front of your readers and perspective readers. You need to love your readers and care for them. They are the most important aspect of your writing. Never let them forget that.

Press Releases

Sending out press releases is a cost-effective way to get out the news about your new book. You can send them to your local news outlets, and send out blast press releases using various services that specialize in sending out press releases. I've received numerous radio and newspaper interviews by using press releases.

In our coaching program, I provide you with your first press release to help you get the word out. You can also do a search for how to write a press release that will help you come up with a good product.

One Last Word

If you don't do this hard work, then you will not succeed as an author, unless just writing and publishing a book is your ultimate goal. If that is you, I want you to aim higher. You never know who is going to fall in love with your book and begin spreading the news.

It is so much easier to be an independent author, and if you can gain some momentum and buzz about your book, it can be financially rewarding. But you will never succeed if you don't try. As I've said numerous times:

"The only guarantee for failure is to not try."

You got this! Now go out there and get it!!